Eleanor Roosevelt: Her Day

S0-AGG-131

Eleanor Roosevelt
Her Day

A Personal Album by
A. David Gurewitsch, M. D.

With an Introduction by Dr. William Korey and the full text
of the Universal Declaration of Human Rights

Foreword by Franklin D. Roosevelt, Jr.

Published by
Quadrangle/The New York Times Book Co.
In cooperation with
The Interchange Foundation

Album of pictures and text
Copyright © 1973, 1974 A. David Gurewitsch, M.D.
Copyright © 1973, 1974 INTERCHANGE Foundation, from
whose earlier edition this edition has been adapted.

All rights reserved, including the right to reproduce this book or portions
thereof in any form. For information, address: Quadrangle/The New York
Times Book Co., 10 East 53 Street, New York, New York 10022. Manufac-
tured in the United States of America. Published simultaneously in Canada
by Fitzhenry & Whiteside, Ltd., Toronto.

Library of Congress Catalog Card Number: 73-90188
International Standard Book Number: 0-8129-0447-8

Acknowledgments

The publication of this book has been made possible by
Milton Charles,
who provided his talents as coordinator, picture editor,
art director and designer;

Gail Ash, associate designer
Maya Yates, editor
Bernard Kass, production

Eleanor Roosevelt Institute

Franklin D. Roosevelt Library, Hyde Park, New York

No one can be perfectly free till all are free;
no one can be perfectly moral till all are moral;
no one can be perfectly happy till all are happy.

Herbert Spencer

Contents

Cover: Eleanor Roosevelt
talks with some Wiltwyck School boys.

Foreword

This is an exciting book, and I wish to express my appreciation to Jean Picker for her thoughtfulness and hard work in bringing together Dr. Korey's article on my mother's role in the creation of the United Nations' Human Rights Declaration with the remarkable photographs taken by David Gurewitsch on many historic occasions and in many parts of the world.

Dr. Korey's piece will remind my generation and will educate the new one of what a profound achievement it was to get almost all the members of the United Nations, with their many and significant differences, to support the Declaration.

David Gurewitsch was my mother's personal physician. He is not only an outstanding member of the medical profession in whose ability and competence my mother had complete confidence and trust, but in these pages he has also demonstrated his remarkable talent as a photographer. David and Edna, his wife, went on many trips to all parts of the world with my mother, and through his constant watch over her health, she was able to maintain the fantastic energy that made it possible for her to do so much. Her traveling companions usually reached the point of exhaustion long before she would ever admit that she was getting a little tired. Through the years, David became not only her faithful doctor but her trusted and loyal friend and, in many ways, occupied the role of a devoted son.

To many of us this book will bring back many memories and will renew our appreciation of my mother's life of dedicated achievement in the interests of people everywhere.

Franklin D. Roosevelt, Jr.

Mrs. Roosevelt addressing a visiting group in the General Assembly hall.

Prologue

A mourner at Eleanor Roosevelt's funeral was overheard saying, "Who will worry about us now that she's left us?"

Everyone who knew Eleanor Roosevelt personally, and everyone who knew her through her writing and public appearances, felt the strength of her friendship—and felt strengthened by it. She had, among many talents, a rare one: she simply claimed everyone's concern as her own.

When Eleanor Roosevelt added to her concern the peoples of the United Nations, she found an international home for this commitment to others. As chairman of the Human Rights Commission, she worked two years to draft the Universal Declaration of Human Rights that was acceptable to diplomats representing millions of people. When the Declaration was unanimously passed by the General Assembly in 1948, its hallmark was—and is today—Eleanor Roosevelt's uncommon concern for humanity.

Twenty-five years have passed since the birth of that historic document. New nations now use the Declaration as cornerstones of their new constitutions. And the thirty rights it honors have become everyday guidelines for governments and eloquent goals to which men and women everywhere aspire.

In the introduction that follows, Dr. William Korey, a specialist in human rights affairs, recounts vivid moments of the Declaration's creation and Eleanor Roosevelt's guiding role in it.

Through the pictures and stories in his personal album, Dr. A. David Gurewitsch—Eleanor Roosevelt's friend, companion and physician—reveals the humanity of Eleanor Roosevelt herself: as an ambassador, as a friend, as a woman, as a mother and head of a family.

Jean Picker, United States Representative to the United Nations Commission for Social Development

Eleanor Roosevelt and the
Universal Declaration of Human Rights

By Dr. William Korey

It was three o'clock in the morning of December 10, 1948, at the Palais de Chaillot in Paris, when the exhausted delegates to the third session of the United Nations General Assembly by a unanimous vote—with only 8 abstaining and 2 absent —adopted the Universal Declaration of Human Rights. What U Thant would call the "Magna Carta of Mankind" and what Alexander Solzhenitsyn would characterize, in his brilliant, undelivered Nobel lecture in 1970, as the "best document" ever produced by the United Nations, was in large measure the product of the energy and imagination of that extraordinary "First Lady of the World," Mrs. Eleanor Roosevelt. The delegates, though weary with fatigue in that early hour twenty-five years ago, were even then acutely aware of how much they—and mankind—were indebted to her leadership. In a tribute, rare in United Nations annals, they rose as one to give her a standing ovation.

Immediately after the Assembly vote, Mrs. Roosevelt jotted down the words "long job finished." The "long job" began on April 29, 1946, in New York. It was the opening meeting of the so-called "nuclear" Commission on Human Rights that was appointed by the U.N. Economic and Social Council to make recommendations about a permanent U.N. human rights body and, more significantly, to consider an "international bill of rights." Mrs. Roosevelt was a logical choice for membership and its chairman.

During the sessions of the permanent U.N. Commission on Human Rights, which began in January,1947, three broad issues emerged. Mrs. Roosevelt played a critical and probably decisive role in the resolution of each of the issues. The first of them—the form of the international bill of rights—was to exert an immediate impact upon the Commission's work. The issue surfaced sharply when the Commission's Drafting Committee met for the first time in June, 1947. Mrs. Roosevelt must have sensed that the form in which the rights would be cast was vital, for she cautioned the Committee that they must prepare a draft that stood some chance of acceptance by all the fifty-eight governments of the U.N. With her encouragement, the Committee decided upon the need to prepare two documents: a Declaration that would constitute a broad set of principles establishing "a common standard of achievement" for all states; and a Convention (or Covenant) that would be legally binding upon contracting parties and carry measures of implementation. She then persuaded Commission members to concentrate initially upon the immediate task of drafting a Declaration.

The second crucial issue was the controversy over what Mrs. Roosevelt called "the relationship of the individual to the state." The Soviet delegate, V.T. Tepliakov, found the rights enumerated in various bills of human rights assembled by the Secretariat totally inapplicable. He would have wanted the deletion of the following: rights to life and of personal liberty; prohibition of slavery and compulsory labor; right to petition national governments and the U.N.; right of property and prohibition of unlawful expropriation; freedom of movement and freedom to resist oppression. The Russian declared that these rights were either superfluous or went beyond the power of the U.N. to establish or impinged upon local customs and the laws of national states.

Mrs. Roosevelt's convictions, however, flowed from a Western historical tradition that found its finest expression in the American Declaration of Independence and Bill of Rights and in the French Declaration of the Rights of Man. In these documents the rights of the individual are held as "anterior and superior" to the state and, as such, are inalienable. This basic premise requires that the state can do nothing more than recognize existing rights and create conditions favorable to their exercise. Her view, despite severe Soviet criticism and dilatory tactics, was to triumph. The Universal Declaration of Human Rights was largely cast in the classical civil libertarian tradition.

Mrs. Roosevelt and Senator John Sherman Cooper.

Mrs. Roosevelt talking with Israel's Golda Meir.

Mrs. Roosevelt chatting with U.S. Ambassador to India Chester Bowles.

Mrs. Roosevelt talking with Sir Zafrullah Khan, Minister of Foreign Affairs of Pakistan.

Mrs. Roosevelt welcomed by a colleague at a U.N. reception.

Mrs. Roosevelt talks with Senator Arthur Vandenberg and U.S. Ambassador Warren Austin.

Composure in the face of considerable Russian provocation was a hallmark of Mrs. Roosevelt's conduct during the commission sessions. Afterwards she would joke about it. In a speech at the Sorbonne in Paris on September 27, 1948, she delighted her audience with the observation that she had been mistaken in thinking that the limits of her patience had been reached in bringing up a large family; in presiding over the Commission on Human Rights, an even greater measure of patience was demanded.

The third great issue that arose at the sessions of the Commission dealt with a group of rights that went considerably beyond the traditional rights of the individual: the new type of social or economic rights. On the one hand, she persuaded a reluctant U.S. State Department to support inclusion of these rights. On the other hand, she recommended that the Declaration set goals for the new type of rights rather than requiring governments to guarantee them immediately. Her opinion was to prevail.

When the Commission's draft moved to the General Assembly in the fall of 1948, the debates became repetitive, interminably long and tedious, and frequently irrelevant (leading Mrs. Roosevelt to complain about the "wordy atmosphere"). Yet they did perform a valuable function. Delegates from differing backgrounds and traditions became involved in a process that fostered a greater understanding of, if not some sympathy for, varying viewpoints. Moreover, the process itself had the effect of assuring a more positive commitment by the representatives of the fifty-eight U.N. members to the principles of the Universal Declaration than might have been the case had there been little or no debate.

For Mrs. Roosevelt, the General Assembly debates constituted not merely a test of her patience; at issue was the question of whether the decisions upon which she and her colleagues in the Commission had labored for so long and with such intensity would be validated. Of necessity, she was cast in the role of defender of the Commission's draft Declaration. Once again, proposals for state encroachment upon or infringement of civil liberties had to be resisted. Once again, detailed obligations upon states to guarantee economic and social rights had to be opposed. And, always, it was essential to avoid provocation. In the face of an incessant verbal assault by the U.S.S.R. delegate upon racial and economic practices in the United States, Mrs. Roosevelt eschewed vituperation, appealing instead for courteousness in debate. "Remember," she told her opponents, "no one who lives in the world is perfect."

In the course of time the Universal Declaration has come to be more than a "declaration of basic principles." A number of legally binding international Conventions on human rights and various peace treaties have incorporated direct reference to the Declaration. In the legislative work of the United Nations, it has become a final arbiter and standard of reference to the Universal Declaration and its provisions in the constitutions of many new states, as is the case in close to twenty African states. Human rights provisions are clearly inspired by the Declaration in the constitutions of a number of other African states as well as new states like Cyprus, Jamaica, and Trinidad and Tobago. Even national courts have made reference to the Declaration and, in several instances, have juridically applied it.

Mrs. Roosevelt must have sensed from the very beginning that the Universal Declaration would become what Dag Hammarskjold later called "a living document." In referring to it as a "Magna Carta," she surely had in mind more than a moral manifesto. The Declaration, like the Magna Carta, would take on a vitality and force that transcended a purely legal definition and defied precise formal description. As early as 1953, she recognized that its "impact on people throughout the world has been of very considerable magnitude, much greater than most Americans suspect."

Mrs. Roosevelt at a Commission meeting.

Eleanor Roosevelt: Her Day

A Personal Album by A. David Gurewitsch, M.D.

A Friendship

I first met Mrs. Roosevelt in 1939 during a reception given by her at the White House. I had the opportunity to speak to her for a minute or two. My recollection of this meeting is that I was in awe of being in the White House and in the presence of this formidable and famous lady. I was deeply impressed by her simplicity and directness. It took close to five years for me to meet her again. This time she was visiting a sick friend, Mrs. Trude Lash, who had been an old friend from student days and who had become one of my first patients in New York. I found Mrs. Roosevelt at her bedside on subsequent medical visits.

Soon after the president's death, Mrs. Roosevelt, having settled in her New York apartment, asked me whether I would be willing to take her as a patient. She smilingly added that she was quite healthy and would probably not take up too much of my time. I readily agreed. Soon afterwards, a rather voluminous record arrived from the National Naval Medical Center in Bethesda, containing her medical data.

On November 27, 1947, I found myself sitting in an airplane heading for Switzerland, next to Mrs. Roosevelt, she for Geneva, as chairman of the United Nations Commission on Human Rights and I for Davos, which then was still famous for the treatment of pulmonary tuberculosis. My purpose was to be cured of a mild case of that condition. When Mrs. Roosevelt first heard about my illness she offered me the stone cottage next to her home in Hyde Park for the prescribed rest cure. I, however, preferred to be treated in the high altitude of the Swiss Alps, where I had been a patient for a short time a good many years before.

This trip to Geneva turned out to be most memorable. The very beginning generated much excitement. As the plane took off, the historic voting at the United Nations General Assembly on the proposed Partition of Palestine had just started. Mrs. Roosevelt had been strongly in favor of Partition and had exerted considerable energy and all her influence to get the United States to vote for it.

A friend had brought a small radio on the plane and our group was listening intensely as one by one, the votes were announced. With great relief we realized that the necessary two-thirds majority in favor of Partition was indeed forthcoming.

In those days this journey to Geneva in a propeller plane was expected to take just short of twenty-four hours. This particular trip however, took four and a half days. We were fogged in in Ireland and we had rather delaying mechanical troubles in Newfoundland. In the absence of the normal ties and obligations usually present in our daily lives, the contact which had gradually grown between Mrs. Roosevelt and myself in the course of the last two and a half years developed a different dimension. The many hours of conversations in the air and especially in Shannon airport resulted in a friendship which was to last throughout the remaining eighteen years of Mrs. Roosevelt's life.

In the detached and somewhat unreal atmosphere of an airplane, I heard much about Mrs. Roosevelt's life and she, in turn, learned about some of the vicissitudes of my life, of my hopes and ambitions.

Mrs. Roosevelt was a most avid and sympathetic listener and questioner. I told her about my background, my extraordinary philosopher father who seemed to have come into this world with one mission only, that of solving the relationship between man and God and man and the world surrounding him. Before the age of ten he had started to explore the thinking of other philosophers, and later concentrated on finding his own personal solution. Time and again he thought that he had reached the answer, only to discover that it was not sufficiently all-inclusive and satisfactory. At the age of twenty-six, however, he felt that he had at last found an adequate solution and with that, the fulfillment of his mission in life. A few months after he had finished developing his philosophy, he drowned in a Swiss lake. This was a few months before I was born. My mother believed firmly that at this point, life did not offer him any further challenge. For her this loss represented a blow from which she never recovered. In her response to a little note I had written her on the occasion of the thirty-fifth anniversary of my father's death, she answered, "Don't you know that for me, every day is the seventh of July?"

I told Mrs. Roosevelt how my mother who had also been a student of philosophy as long as her husband was alive, abandoned this field after his death to study medicine. She became a practitioner of the healing art and developed a method of massage, accomplishing extraordinary results.

I told Mrs. Roosevelt about my mother's strength of character, how she managed to educate her two sons, to keep her family together as enemy aliens in Germany during the First World War, to meet the blow of poverty which followed the Russian Revolution and to escape the Hitler persecutions. My determination to become a doctor was postponed because of my belief that I could not put such a heavy financial burden on my mother. I had been unable to follow her deep religious approach to life which gave her the certainty that if something was right for a person, means would be found with which to accomplish it, and that my worries about financial support were unwarranted. Hindsight proved that my mother's conviction had been right and that the seven or eight years I spent trying to finance my medical studies were really not essential. However, the means I acquired in this effort allowed me to pursue a rather independent, and long-term education, taking me to renowned teaching centers.

Although we both had come from different parts of the world and from different backgrounds, it developed that Mrs. Roosevelt and I had much in common. We both had grown up fatherless. During our impressionable young years, we both had been raised by grandparents. We both had feelings of early deprivation. The sense of "service" had been strongly instilled into us, and accomplishment in life was to be measured more in service than in "happiness." Each of us was shy, felt somewhat "outside" of the established norms, and essentially lonely.

In spite of having been born into the "establishment," the niece of a President, the wife of a President, Mrs. Roosevelt was basically a "deprived" person. It began with the separation from her beloved father, was continued by his early death and by the early loss of her mother. In her most impressionable years, she was brought up by a stern grandmother. She found her main emotional support in a French teacher in a school in England. This feeling of homelessness was repeated to a degree during her marriage, when her domineering mother-in-law's house never quite seemed her own.

In Shannon, at that time, sleeping quarters in the event of flight delays were located in barracks over a mile away from the airport dining room. The distance had to be covered on foot. Mrs. Roosevelt took it upon herself to provide me with the necessary food while I, ill, remained in the barracks during the three days of our delay there. Her interpretation of "help" was overwhelming. She read to me, and our conversations continued. By the time the plane arrived in Geneva the doctor-patient relationship had become a real friendship.

Throughout Mrs. Roosevelt's stay in Geneva, the close contact continued by telephone and daily correspondence, and was not interrupted by her return home. When I got back and resumed my own work once more, my family and I, as a matter of course, became part of Mrs. Roosevelt's intimate circle. I grew to know her children and grandchildren and was gradually drawn more and more into the vibrating atmosphere created by Mrs. Roosevelt and her surroundings.

My incentive for taking photographs was no different from that of any lay photographer. The recording of a sight, event, person, supplements a diary. My pictures are not aimed at posterity and they certainly were never meant to inconvenience the people being photographed. Mrs. Roosevelt was one of the world's most photographed persons and I, for one, was determined not to add, in her private life, the unavoidable strain produced by ever-present photographers. I also avoided the glare and possible discomfort of artificial light.

For a long time my photographs essentially covered whatever we saw together. This meant that Mrs. Roosevelt was not in the picture. Gradually Mrs. Roosevelt encouraged me to include her into pictures taken, assuring me that she did not mind.

This book is meant to offer some glimpses of Mrs. Roosevelt in her later years. It is my hope that it will allow the reader to relate in a more personal way to a great human being. Perhaps it may add insight into a complicated and strong personality, whose stature I feel has yet to be adequately measured. History will judge Mrs. Roosevelt's greatness. As with all people, the more known about them, the more accurate the appraisal.

Mrs. Roosevelt and the author.

At Home

For Mrs. Roosevelt, Hyde Park was home. From whatever distance, and for however short a time, she would go back there. Time and again she said that she envisaged retiring there, sitting in a rocking chair and knitting.

Mrs. Roosevelt's cottage, Val-Kill, a few miles from the imposing main residence, the "Big House," consisted of several parts joined together which originally housed a furniture factory. Each section seemed small, and Val-Kill looked unimpressive from the outside. But the interior was roomy and comfortable—bedrooms for at least a dozen guests, living and dining rooms, a library, a big country kitchen, spacious porches. In one living room where Mrs. Roosevelt had her desk, we assembled for drinks before lunch and dinner. She often sat at her desk then, seemingly oblivious to the conversation that went on around her, reading her mail or making notations on how letters should be answered.

But at all times Mrs. Roosevelt made her guests feel at home and made them feel that their presence did not interfere in the slightest with what she wanted or had to do. She was an ideal hostess. Her guests were left to do almost entirely as they liked; they were just expected to appear for meals. She saw to the smallest details, making sure each guest's room had all the necessary comforts as well as freshly picked flowers, cookies, or fruit, and possibly books that would be of interest to a particular guest. When she wrote out the menus every morning for the cook, she knew everyone's food preferences. She made sure to shop herself for such seasonal delicacies as melons or fresh corn that she had spotted in the country stores. Whether there were ten guests or a hundred, close friends or visiting royalty, she never enlarged her small staff or altered her style of preparing for the day's events.

What Mrs. Roosevelt enjoyed most at Hyde Park was being with people she loved. There was usually a son or two with his family, or her brother Hall's daughter and her children. And a few friends: her secretary, Malvina Thompson, and later, Maureen Corr; Lorena Hickok, the AP reporter assigned to cover Mrs. Roosevelt during the White House years; writer Joseph Lash and his wife Trude, my wife Edna, and I. Laura Delano, her husband's first cousin, was a frequent visitor as were her literary agent, Nannine Joseph; President Roosevelt's Secretary of the Treasury, Henry Morganthau, Jr., and his wife Marcelle; and her lawyer, Henry Hooker, who was a former law partner of FDR. There were many more familiar faces, and usually surprises: royalty, prime ministers, visiting groups of United Nations representatives from all corners of the world, Russian jurists, American political and labor figures.

Mrs. Roosevelt stands in the portico of the Big House.

Mrs. Roosevelt follows Tamas, a descendant of her husband's famous Fala, on a Hyde Park walk.

Whatever the season and however busy her schedule, Mrs. Roosevelt took time for hour-long walks in Hyde Park's lovely woodlands. As a rule she walked every day she was there, either with a friend or with one of her Scottish terriers. In company, she enjoyed the chance for quiet conversation; alone, she might use the time to resolve a problem or to make a decision about some future plans.

At Home

In her garden, Mrs. Roosevelt cuts some marigolds that she will carefully arrange in her home.

Mrs. Roosevelt loved flowers in her house, and she regularly picked them for her Val-Kill rooms. She also brought them back with her for her home in New York, for friends' homes, or for someone she knew who was sick in a hospital. She disliked receiving as a gift such formal displays as an orchid corsage but was touched if a friend brought her a single garden rose or a few field daisies.

At Home

After a swim, Mrs. Roosevelt stretches out on the lawn—a rare moment of utter inactivity.

In the summer, just before lunch or in the late afternoon, Mrs. Roosevelt usually swam in the pool near her cottage. Occasionally she dived from the board. Each time I saw her about to dive, I was impressed by her expression of dislike: she would hold her nose with one hand and look grimly determined. Once I asked her why she dived if it was so obviously uncomfortable. She answered, "It is good for my character."

At Home

Hyde Park weekends brought together a constantly changing group of lively Roosevelts.

Mrs. Roosevelt particularly liked to have her Val-Kill home crowded with members of her large family. Above, from left to right at the dining table with her, are grandson Haven; daughter Anna; son Franklin, Jr.; and Sue, Franklin's wife at the time. At top left, she sits and chats with Anna and Anna's son, Curtis. Bottom left, she enjoys a relaxed after-dinner conversation with her son, James.

With Family and Friends

At the marriage of her niece, Mrs. Roosevelt greets some family members of the wedding.

Mrs. Roosevelt was very fond of her brother's daughter Eleanor, whose marriage to George Roach took place at Hyde Park. With Mrs. Roosevelt, from left to right, are grandson Haven; Mrs. John Cutter, mother of the bride; Stewart Elliott, the bride's son from a former marriage; and the newlyweds.

With Family and Friends

Mrs. Roosevelt glows in her favorite role: as mother, grandmother, and great-grandmother.

The four generations of Roosevelt ladies pictured here on a Hyde Park weekend all have in common the names Anna Eleanor. Standing with Mrs. Roosevelt are her daughter Anna on the left, Anna's daughter "Sisty" on the right, and the youngest of the group, Sisty's daughter Eleanor.

With Family and Friends

Mrs. Roosevelt relaxes with longtime friends Lorena Hickok, left, and Nannine Joseph, above.

Personal relationships meant more to Mrs. Roosevelt than public activities, and she liked having close friends with her at Val-Kill. Her friendship with Lorena Hickok began during White House days when, as an AP reporter, "Hick" was the first member of the press ever assigned to cover a president's wife. At this time Hick is an invalid, retired to the village of Hyde Park, and Mrs. Roosevelt looked after her with characteristic loyalty and affection. Nannine Joseph, another long-standing friend, was first FDR's and later Mrs. Roosevelt's literary agent.

**With
Family
and
Friends**

Above, with her cook and housekeeper, Marge Entrup.

Mrs. Roosevelt was as devoted to members of her staff as they were to her. Mrs. Entrup grew accustomed to hearing Mrs. Roosevelt say on Hyde Park evenings, "Marge, only seventeen people for breakfast tomorrow."

Left, with my daughter, Maria, here ten weeks old.

Maria was the littlest Hyde Park guest during one summer. Her hostess inscribed another print of this picture for her: "To Maria Anna, with love from one of her most staunch admirers! Eleanor Roosevelt."

With Family and Friends

Left, Lyndon B. Johnson gives a Memorial Day speech. Above, in the audience are Trude and Joseph Lash.

Holidays in Hyde Park were special occasions because Mrs. Roosevelt's enthusiastic celebration of them in traditional family style generated an atmosphere of excitement.

Memorial Day was particularly respected by Mrs. Roosevelt. She, or one of her children, invited a prominent person to speak at FDR's grave in the Rose Garden. A platform was erected for speakers, important guests, and the Roosevelt family, and several hundred other guests sat in folding chairs on the lawn. The ceremony was presided over by Arthur Smith, the postmaster of Hyde Park and president of the Roosevelt Home Club, and opened by a local talent singing the national anthem. After Senate Majority Leader Lyndon Johnson spoke here, local Boy Scouts passed the audience and solemnly carried a flag to the grave, where wreaths were laid and a Scout played taps.

As I remember, Mrs. Roosevelt never missed being on that platform in the Rose Garden after her husband's death. And of the many Memorial Day ceremonies I attended, I do not remember once when it rained.

Hyde Park Holidays

Lyndon B. Johnson honors FDR on Memorial Day.

After Senator Johnson delivered his speech in the Rose Garden, the family, dignitaries, and an array of guests moved here near the FDR Library, where the Senator planted a tree in memory of President Roosevelt. Mrs. Roosevelt—her son James and his wife at the time stand behind her—and the others are listening to Reverend Gordon Kidd, the pastor of Hyde Park's St. James Church (on the right with his back to the camera) closing the ceremony with a benediction.

Hyde Park Holidays

49

On another Memorial Day occasion, Adlai Stevenson gets some last-minute advice and does some final editing of his speech.

Mrs. Roosevelt always welcomed the chance to see and talk with Adlai Stevenson. Longtime friends and loyal admirers of each other's activities, they shared deep interests in both national politics and international affairs. At the time of this Memorial Day speech, Mr. Stevenson was Ambassador to the United Nations. His efforts to work toward safeguarding and strengthening the world organization found Mrs. Roosevelt again being his ardent supporter.

**Hyde
Park
Holidays**

On the Fourth of July, above, James Roosevelt reads the Declaration of Independence to a gathering of family and friends. At right, chauffeur "Tubby" Curnan and Mrs. Roosevelt lead the Hyde Park parade.

Every Fourth of July, Mrs. Roosevelt or one of her sons read the Declaration of Independence to the crowd assembled for an informal outdoor lunch. On that day she sometimes headed the parade in the village of Hyde Park: she and oversize Tubby especially enhanced the holiday spectacle when they appeared in her tiny Fiat (at the time, her son, Franklin, had the Fiat franchise in the United States and had persuaded his mother to buy the car).

Hyde Park Holidays

A Thanksgiving dinner, above, gets underway as soon as Mrs. Roosevelt proposes her toast, right.

The large dining table at Mrs. Roosevelt's cottage looked even more sumptuous than usual on Thanksgiving Day. Family and friends around the table here are, from left to right: granddaughter Nina; Joseph Lash; my wife Edna; grandson Curtis's wife then, Ruth; grandson Haven, and Henry Osthagen, a friend of Malvina Thompson, Mrs. Roosevelt's secretary. On this and all other festive occasions throughout the year, Mrs. Roosevelt offered one toast: "To the United States of America. To the President. To those we love who are not with us today."

Hyde Park Holidays

The lavish Christmas dinner, above, is matched by lavish piles of presents in the living room, right.

Christmas was the highlight of the Hyde Park year, and Mrs. Roosevelt began preparing for it virtually on January 2. Wherever she traveled she bought presents—maple sugar in Vermont, salad bowls in Pennsylvania, costumed dolls in Greece, silks in India. And every purchase was clearly labeled in her mind for a particular person.

When we woke up on Christmas morning, everybody staying at Val-Kill—family, a few friends, one or two foreign guests —found at his or her bedroom door a large stocking that Mrs. Roosevelt had stuffed with sweets and good-luck pieces. By one thirty in the afternoon we had gathered in Mrs. Roosevelt's study, with the fireplace blazing and cards crowded on the mantel. In the dining room the huge table, set with infinite care, was a wonderful sight. Decorations nearly covered it. Each place card, handwritten by Mrs. Roosevelt with a verse or drawing appropriate to the person, was surrounded by small presents as well as fruit, nuts, and chocolate. When we were seated and her grandsons had filled the champagne glasses, Mrs. Roosevelt rose and proposed her standard toast.

**Hyde
Park
Holidays**

After the meal almost everyone knew what awaited behind the closed doors of the living room. A Christmas tree stood in the corner, but there were so many presents that they were piled on a separate chair for each person. Mrs. Roosevelt's mountain of gifts stood near the porch door—gifts from people in the room and from people all over the world.

As we unwrapped our packages, Mrs. Roosevelt moved from person to person—anxious, excited, happy—watching while we opened something she especially wanted us to have. "Do you like it? Does it fit? Is the color right?" After we finished, and after the wrapping paper was cleared away or burned, Mrs. Roosevelt read aloud from Dickens's *A Christmas Carol*.

Only after everyone's excitement about his or her own presents had died down did Mrs. Roosevelt begin opening her own gifts. As she unwrapped each one, what counted was the donor rather than the gift. In the years I knew her, objects meant little to her. What was important was the person from whom an object came. If the person was close to her, she would like the present, use it, have it on display. She would wear the same scarf or use the same pocketbook for a long time if it had been given to her by somebody she loved.

**Hyde
Park
Holidays**

Schoolchildren listen intently to Mrs. Roosevelt's stories about the Big House.

Mrs. Roosevelt loved to take visitors around the main Roosevelt residence at Hyde Park, the Big House. In her personal way she brought to life the past events that made each room historic. Among her favorite guests were children, and her concern for their well-being everywhere was highlighted one day when she toured the Big House and the FDR Library with the Shah of Persia. As she pointed out to the Shah the Persian rug he had once given FDR, the Shah—eager to tell her details about it—said that the stitching was so fine only the tiny hands of children could work it. Mrs. Roosevelt was upset by such child labor and repeated this story frequently.

Visitors at Hyde Park

Val-Kill visitors: above, members of the American Association for the United Nations; left, Walter Reuther with Mrs. Roosevelt, her grandson Haven, and her daughter Anna.

Mrs. Roosevelt particularly enjoyed talking with people interested in the United Nations. After she was no longer a delegate to the U.N., she transferred her interest in international affairs to involvement with the A.A.U.N. With Mr. Reuther she shared thinking about another deep interest: social and labor affairs. On weekend visits the dynamic labor leader told stories about the early days of the United Automobile Workers and shared his ideas on such subjects as automation and the use of leisure time.

**Visitors at
Hyde Park**

At her cottage Mrs. Roosevelt has her first talk with Presidential nominee John F. Kennedy.

This meeting came about in connection with the Senator's invitation to address the New York Association of Senior Citizens at the Hyde Park estate. Before Senator Kennedy agreed to speak, he asked for a meeting with Mrs. Roosevelt, feeling that it would be politically unwise to appear at Hyde Park if he would be snubbed by her.

Ever since his nomination, Senator Kennedy had tried to meet with Mrs. Roosevelt, hoping to persuade her to support his campaign. He was aware, of course, of her forceful advocacy of Adlai Stevenson and her many concerns about his own qual-

Visitors at Hyde Park

ifications—his youth and the influence of Catholicism were among these concerns. But after his nomination he had made a number of speeches clarifying subjects that worried Mrs. Roosevelt, and her attitude had softened. She agreed to invite him to lunch on the day of his Hyde Park speech.

It turned out that the day before this lunch date a granddaughter, John Roosevelt's child Sally, fell from a horse while at an upstate New York camp. On learning the news, Mrs. Roosevelt drove to the distant hospital. Sally could not be saved and died during the night. Mrs. Roosevelt returned home early in the morning. Despite the tragedy and despite only a few hours' sleep, she felt bound to honor her appointment, even though Senator Kennedy offered to cancel it.

Visitors at Hyde Park

At left, Mrs. Roosevelt and John F. Kennedy after their informal Val-Kill discussion. Above, Senator Kennedy delivering his speech at Hyde Park.

The result of the first meeting between Mrs. Roosevelt and Presidential nominee John F. Kennedy is clearly evident here in both their faces as they are leaving her living room. Senator Kennedy gave his speech to an enormous crowd, and when he left Hyde Park, remarked he was "absolutely smitten by this woman." Following this meeting, Mrs. Roosevelt gradually warmed to the candidate, taking an increasingly active role in his campaign.

**Visitors at
Hyde Park**

The Khrushchevs visit Hyde Park.

When Soviet Chairman Nikita Khrushchev and his wife Nina returned Mrs. Roosevelt's earlier visit to their Yalta home, they arrived late, with little time left before the Chairman's scheduled appearance at the United Nations. After a brief tour there was no time to eat the lavish meal Mrs. Roosevelt had readied. The only unhurried moment came when she poured champagne and proposed a toast for friendship between their two governments. Ready to drink to that, Mr. Khrushchev said, "They call me a dictator. You see how little power I have? I told my wife not to drink any alcohol and in front of me she takes champagne." Then he went to the table laden with food and took a dry roll "for the road."

Visitors at Hyde Park

Yugoslavia's Tito returns a call.

Mrs. Roosevelt had previously spent some time with President Tito at his summer home on the Adriatic island of Brioni. There, as at her cottage here, she found the Yugoslav leader to be an urbane, sharply intelligent companion and conversationalist. They take this opportunity to exchange ideas on the different politics of their two countries and the difficult cold-war stalemate of international relations.

**Visitors at
Hyde Park**

Ethiopian royalty comes to Hyde Park.

On two separate occasions members of the Ethiopian royal family visited Mrs. Roosevelt at Val-Kill. At the top of this page she talks with the wife of Crown Prince Mered Azmach Asfa Wossen. Above, John Roosevelt chats with the Crown Prince.

When Emperor Haile Selassie visited Hyde Park, at right, Mrs. Roosevelt was asked in advance to make sure that His Majesty

Visitors at Hyde Park

had a chance to rest and wash up immediately after his arrival. But these amenities were accomplished in a hurry because the Emperor wanted to look at television. He had been interviewed by children the day before, and the taped TV program was scheduled to be shown just after his lunchtime arrival. He had never seen himself on TV and was eager to watch how he appeared in the interview. While his party stood at a respectful distance, he made himself comfortable on a stool facing the TV, casually taking off his shoes a moment after he sat down.

Visitors at Hyde Park

Emperor Haile Selassie salutes FDR.

After the Emperor's informal visit with Mrs. Roosevelt at her cottage, he accompanies her on a tour of the Big House at Hyde Park. At right, standing in the Rose Garden by FDR's grave, he pays formal respects to the late President, his formidable wartime ally.

Visitors at Hyde Park

Mrs. Roosevelt, with my mother on the left, tells a story to a crowd of Wiltwyck boys.

As a sponsor of the Wiltwyck School for disturbed boys, Mrs. Roosevelt looked forward to the day each year when the children came to Hyde Park for a picnic. They too looked forward to the outdoor occasion, and each of them knew the one big rule of the day: no "lifting" from Mrs. Roosevelt.

A certain ritual grew up around the picnic day. Before lunch the boys played on the lawn at Val-Kill. Then they stood in

**Wiltwyck
Picnic**

line for the huge quantities of hot dogs, beans, cole slaw, Cokes, milk, and ice cream, which Mrs. Roosevelt always helped serve. After eating, the children would gather around Mrs. Roosevelt, who then read them stories by Rudyard Kipling or told stories of her own.

My mother was hard of hearing, as was Mrs. Roosevelt, and here she sits close by, intently following every word. The two ladies had a deep mutual admiration, sharing much in common: both had spent a lifetime in the service of people, both were eager to learn, and both sought contact with youth.

Wiltwyck Picnic

Above, Eddie Brown finds a friend.

At one of the Wiltwyck picnics, a boy approached Mrs. Roosevelt and asked, ''Mrs. Roosevelt, what is my name?'' ''I don't know,'' she said, ''what *is* your name?'' ''Eddie Brown. Will you remember?'' Five or ten minutes later the same boy was back with the same question: ''What is my name?'' This time Mrs. Roosevelt gave him the desired answer. After a little while he returned once more and again repeated his question, just as I took this picture.

**Wiltwyck
Picnic**

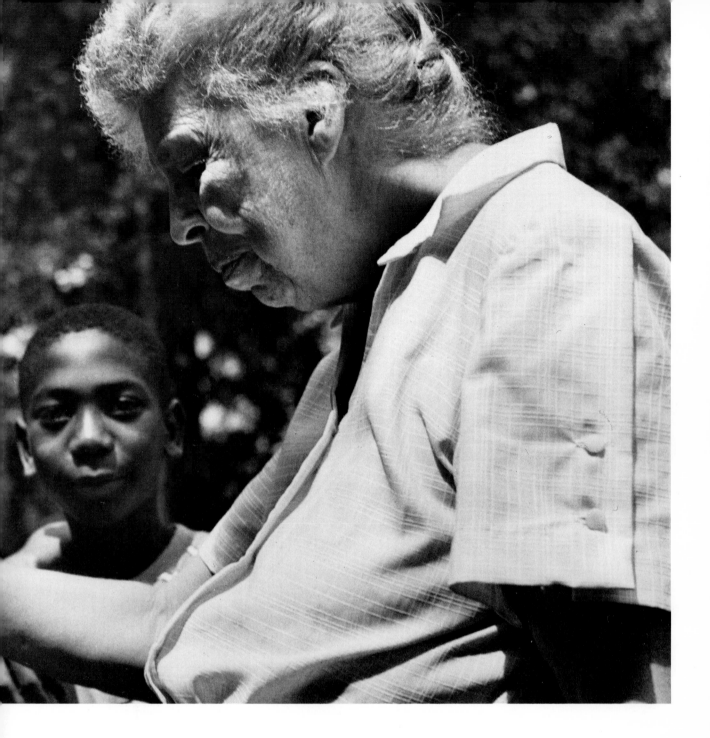

Next page: Harry Belafonte meets Wiltwyck boys.

When Mrs. Roosevelt learned that the Wiltwyck boys idolized Harry Belafonte, she invited him to Hyde Park. He immediately became interested in the boys and their school. He paid for the hiring of a Jamaican musician to teach them to play steel drums and agreed to give an annual concert at Carnegie Hall for the school's benefit. Once the steel-band members had perfected their playing, the boys accompanied Mr. Belafonte at this musical event.

**Wiltwyck
Picnic**

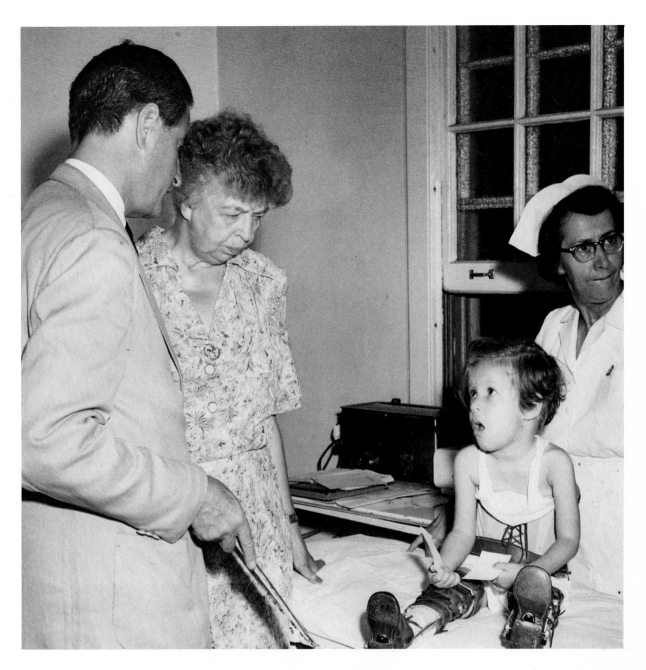

Above, Mrs. Roosevelt and I chat with a child at Blythedale Children's Hospital in Valhalla, New York.

Always interested in children, Mrs. Roosevelt accompanied me on several occasions to Blythedale, a model institution for the care of handicapped children. I have been associated with Blythedale for years as medical director.

Excursions

Left, Mrs. Belafonte and Mrs. Roosevelt stand by while Harry Belafonte tries his hand at archery.

Mr. Belafonte's visit to Hyde Park coincided with a meeting there of the local archery club. The singer's enthusiastic interest in the Wiltwyck boys is here temporarily set aside by an eagerness to see if he can handle a bow and arrow.

Wiltwyck Picnic

A trip to Woodstock, Vermont.

To Mrs. Roosevelt, any excuse for a picnic was a good excuse, and she planned outdoor meals in banquet size and style. Above, on an outing to Vermont, she readies a typically lavish spread. We were on our way to visit my daughter, Grania, then attending the Woodstock Country School. At left, Grania shows Mrs. Roosevelt the school's kitchen and proudly introduces her to some of its staff.

Excursions

At a Warm Springs ceremony Mrs. Roosevelt joins in honoring eminent scientists in polio research.

Georgia's Warm Springs was a favorite retreat of President Roosevelt. He went there to rest, to get treatments for his polio affliction, and ultimately to build a polio research center. Representing her husband's contribution to polio research, here Mrs. Roosevelt is with some of the people whose work led to the

discovery of the polio vaccine. Each is standing beneath his or her bronze bust. Included are Dr. Albert Sabin, at the extreme left, and Dr. Jonas Salk, to the left of Mrs. Roosevelt. To her right is Basil O'Connor, co-founder, with FDR, of the National Foundation for Infantile Paralysis and at this time its president. Mr. O'Connor and his organization were responsible for this tribute and for the sponsorship of the scientists pictured here.

Excursions

Mrs. Roosevelt talks with Arthur Schlesinger, Jr., below, at the 1960 Democratic National Convention. At right, she arrives for one of the convention meetings.

Mrs. Roosevelt worked hard at the Los Angeles convention to support Adlai Stevenson as a Presidential candidate. She addressed many state delegations and held a press conference at which she strongly urged Stevenson's nomination while Mr. Schlesinger spoke just as firmly for his Presidential choice John F. Kennedy.

Of all the happenings during those politically hectic days, I particularly remember Mrs. Roosevelt's first arrival at Convention Hall. As she hurried to her seat in the front row of the first balcony, a gradually increasing ovation for her arose in the enormous auditorium. By the time she reached her seat,

the thousands of delegates had stood up, turned around, and were applauding and shouting.

Mrs. Roosevelt paid no attention to this commotion. She sat down quickly and immediately busied herself with her pocketbook. Sitting next to her, I was stunned by her reaction and whispered to her, "Don't you see what's going on?" but she continued to inspect her pocketbook. Finally, when the applause would not stop, she half raised herself, made a small gesture to the crowd, and quickly sat down again. After a while, when the noise had calmed down and the convention proceedings had resumed, I asked her why she had been reluctant to acknowledge such an impressive reception. "But don't you see," she said, "any encouragement of the applause would have been impolite to the speaker."

Excursions

Mrs. Roosevelt returns to Campobello.

On her last excursion to Campobello, the family summer retreat for so many years, Mrs. Roosevelt continued to work at everyday chores like reading her mail, above. But she also delighted in organizing picnics and driving to the island places she liked best. One secluded spot she particularly loved could only be reached on foot. Although no longer an agile walker, she was determined to show it to her secretary, Maureen Corr, my wife Edna, and me. We made our way off a path and, with some difficulty, pushed through thick underbrush and over soft ground to the tree at the left, where Maureen took this picture.

Excursions

The wall of Mrs. Roosevelt's bedroom in her New York house
mirrored her desire to be surrounded by people she loved—the
pictures are of family and friends.

At Home

On Travels Abroad

On her travels as well as at home, Mrs. Roosevelt kept a strenuous schedule. But on the many trips that I accompanied her on, she was seldom ill and her remarkable constitution usually left her with energy to spare. She was helped in this by the rare ability to relax instantly and completely. Between appointments and destinations, in cars, planes, or hotel rooms, she could catnap and wake up refreshed. Wherever she traveled and however full the day's schedule, she always finished what needed to be done that day, whether it was writing her column, "My Day," reading her mail, or writing letters home.

Mrs. Roosevelt's eagerness to learn—from people she met and from places she visited—made travel for her a constant delight and stimulation. She enjoyed both planning and undertaking trips. When travel destinations were agreed upon, she arranged for the journey in a thorough, efficient way, even foreseeing contingencies that might arise. Of course some plans depended on her hosts or the local circumstances, but her scheduling allowed for this, along with impromptu excursions.

Among the few unpredictable aspects of Mrs. Roosevelt's travels that I remember were her eating habits. When free from official lunches and dinners, where she felt courtesy demanded her to eat fully, she might decide to go on a diet which consisted of eating just salads or else practically nothing. Once, in Paris during a United Nations session, she invited some colleagues to dinner at a restaurant where, unknown to her, a gastronomical society was dining that evening. Her party was received with great ceremony and, without asking what she would like to eat, the proprietor proposed a long list of exquisite dishes. When he paused for breath, Mrs. Roosevelt—who was in one of her determined dieting periods—politely said, "Please give me scrambled eggs." Yet shortly afterward, at another fine Parisian restaurant, she ate all the special delicacies offered. On this occasion the proprietress was politely determined: honored to have such a distinguished guest, she charged only one franc for the meal and could not be persuaded to change the bill. Mrs. Roosevelt left a tip of 100,000 francs.

As an experienced traveler and observer, Mrs. Roosevelt knew that studying a few subjects in depth in a foreign country could reveal many insights into its life and spirit. To her primary interests in education and social services, she added medical care when we traveled together. She thought travel in a foreign country, especially one with a totally different culture, was like a jigsaw puzzle with thousands of separate pieces. She knew that even the most conscientious and industrious visitor could collect only a limited number of pieces and could make many mistakes trying to place them where they belonged.

My travels with Mrs. Roosevelt began with a month-long trip to India. Over a period of ten years I accompanied her on journeys to some twenty countries, including the Soviet Union, which we visited twice. What follows are a few glimpses of Mrs. Roosevelt on some of these trips.

Mrs. Roosevelt visits a maharaja.

The one maharaja Mrs. Roosevelt planned to visit in India was the imposing Jam Sahib, above at the right, a colleague at the United Nations. He entertained her lavishly at his palace in Jamnagar. He also took her on a tour of neighboring villages where, honoring what was then a relatively new law, he shook hands with untouchables. Here he stops in a decorative tent to greet and talk with them.

India

New Delhi garden parties, like the one above, welcome Mrs. Roosevelt to India. Prime Minister Jawaharlal Nehru is standing at the left, and his sister, Madame Vijaya Pandit, is sitting behind the tea table. Right, Mrs. Roosevelt addresses members of the Indian Parliament, with Prime Minister Nehru, chin in hand, listening thoughtfully.

As a guest of the government in India, Mrs. Roosevelt had a full travel schedule and was quickly immersed in the sharp contrasts within India. Her formal introduction to Indians came at garden parties on her arrival, crowded with notables that included jeweled maharajas and ladies in beautiful saris. Not long after these splendid receptions, Mrs. Roosevelt visited a little hut near New Delhi that Gandhi had once used. Inside was a rolled-up straw mat, a spinning wheel and—hanging on a nail—a handwoven loincloth. Nothing else. Mrs. Roosevelt commented: "How little a human being really needs."

At the time of Mrs. Roosevelt's visit, India was newly independent and deeply committed to a neutral position both in world affairs and in the cold war. As an American, Mrs. Roosevelt was in an officially sensitive political atmosphere, and the members of Parliament that she was scheduled to address were aloof and almost hostile.

India

U.S. Ambassador Chester Bowles had briefed her for the occasion, advising her what to avoid talking about. The list seemed endless and finally Mrs. Roosevelt asked, "Then what am I allowed to speak about?" The Ambassador said, "Oh, you will know." She asked Mr. Nehru how long he thought her speech should be. He answered, "This is your occasion. As long as you want." "Would thirty minutes be all right?" she asked. Mr. Nehru shrugged and said, "Any time you feel is right."

Wearing a simple dress, comfortable walking shoes, and a flowery hat, Mrs. Roosevelt walked onto the Parliament platform and, without notes, gave a chatty, warm, simple speech. She did not defend the United States. She said she understood the Indian position of aloofness, for after all the United States had been just as aloof before World War I, wanting to avoid other peoples' squabbles. Also, the United States had not long ago been a new country that had freed itself from the British, then built up its own policies. Nobody, she said, could understand the Indian attitude better than she could.

After some five minutes of her talk there was a little scattered applause. After a few more minutes the applause grew. After some twenty minutes Mrs. Roosevelt had the icy audience warmed to her—and to her country. And exactly at the end of thirty minutes she finished her talk.

India

Agra's Taj Mahal keeps a promise to Mrs. Roosevelt.

Of all the lavish palaces, temples, mosques, and shrines Mrs. Roosevelt saw on her India travels, none affected her more deeply than seeing the Taj Mahal.

As a girl, Mrs. Roosevelt had received a letter from her father —whom she loved very much and who died when she was eight years old—that said, "Little Nell, when you grow up you must go and see the Taj Mahal on a night of the full moon. There is a bench not far away, next to one of the lotus-leaf basins, where you should sit and contemplate."

Her visit to Agra was planned to coincide with the appearance of a full moon. Despite her father's words and perhaps because of the expectation she had held for so many years, Mrs. Roosevelt had prepared herself to be disappointed by the shrine. But the approach to it, the proportions of its architecture, its lotus ponds, the arrangement of its steps—everything overwhelmed her. For her it was a perfect monument, wonderful in daylight and still more breathtaking in moonlight, at right, when she sat on the bench described by her father.

India

In Israel, Mrs. Roosevelt visits a center for children, above, and an Arab sheik, right.

Mrs. Roosevelt's first visit to Israel deeply affected her and she returned whenever she could. Apart from her work in the United Nations, where she had fought for the creation of Israel, her life was devoted to solving human problems. Here she found a new nation tackling society's old problems with enormous energy, creativity, and determination. In Israel, it seemed to her, nothing was impossible.

Israel

Wherever she went—to the cities, to a kibbutz, to the immigration camps—she eagerly listened to Israelis talking about their emerging life-styles. Near Beersheba she met an Arab sheik (standing in the center of the picture above) with at least two distinctions: he had remained neutral during all Israeli conflicts, and he had a large harem. His instant regard for Mrs. Roosevelt prompted him to propose marriage to her. She asked jokingly what number wife she would be. When he replied that she would be thirty-seven, she smiled and—always the diplomat—gracefully declined his offer.

Israel

The David Ben-Gurions entertain Mrs. Roosevelt.

Of all the spirited people she met in Israel, Mrs. Roosevelt was most struck by Prime Minister David Ben-Gurion, remembering his penetrating eyes, which were always alert and sparkling when he spoke or listened. Despite his prominence, he lived with his wife Paula in a very small house in Tel Aviv. And his living room was constantly becoming smaller: its walls were lined with books, and as the number grew, shelves were built in front of shelves, three deep like library stacks. The Prime Minister had read them all and knew where each one was located. Mrs. Roosevelt spent some time looking at what subjects he read: his largest collections were in ancient history and in Greek philosophy.

Israel

Mrs. Roosevelt relishes sight-seeing in Greece.

With no official duties scheduled for her Greece trip, Mrs. Roosevelt bent her considerable energies toward seeing traditionally famous places. Above, she explores the ancient Greek arts perfected in the Athenian Acropolis. At left, with her secretary, Maureen Corr, she buys some modern Greek crafts —handwoven towels—at a village bazaar, always mindful of her long Christmas-present list.

Greece

Mrs. Roosevelt lunches with an American archeologist in Athens, above, and views the imposing mountain scenery of Delphi with Maureen Corr, left.

Mrs. Roosevelt was accompanied by archeologists on much of her Greek sight-seeing. Their knowledgeable stories of Greek history and legend fascinated her. Above, she listens intently to the archeologist who, at the time of her visit, was in charge of excavating Athens' ancient meeting place, the Agora. At Delphi, the awesome landscape suited what was perhaps the world's first international meeting place: here members of different, often antagonistic, Greek city-states could peacefully gather to hear Apollo's oracular wisdom.

Greece

Yugoslavia's Tito tours his island homes.

Mrs. Roosevelt's first trip to an iron-curtain country, Yugoslavia, was climaxed by a visit with President Tito on the Adriatic island of Brioni, the summer residence of the Yugoslav head of state. President Tito, above left, leads a party, which includes his wife, Jovanka, beside Mrs. Roosevelt, along the pier below his official residence. From here he took Mrs. Roosevelt for a quick spin in the powerboat, below left. Later we boarded a small yacht, above, to cruise to his nearby private island. As part of stringent security measures, our yacht was surrounded by destroyers. When children from summer camps along the shore realized their President was in the center of this impressive naval custody, thousands of them lined the beaches shouting, "Tito! Tito!"

Yugoslavia

The Titos and Mrs. Roosevelt have spirited talks.

Throughout the two-day visit, Mrs. Roosevelt talked lengthily with the Titos. Among the topics Mrs. Tito, above, spoke of was education, as she had recently completed her university studies that had been interrupted by her partisan activities in World War II. With the President, at right, in the stone cottage on his private little island, discussions focused on political affairs. Mrs. Roosevelt listened intently to the President's review of his country's brand of communism. She was impressed by his concern for his people, his reasoned ideas, and his alert intelligence, later referring to him as a "practical person" and a forceful "doer."

Yugoslavia

In Hong Kong, Mrs. Roosevelt visits a palm reader.

Like most visitors to Hong Kong, Mrs. Roosevelt spent some time shopping there, mostly for Christmas gifts. On one of our shopping excursions we stopped at this fortune teller's stall so he could read our hands. Of course he had no idea who Mrs. Roosevelt was; to him she was just one of thousands of tourists. He was taken aback when he saw her palm: he said this was an extraordinary and powerful lady who had done great things. When he came to my hand, he said I was going to make discoveries and do important things. As we left, Mrs. Roosevelt's comment was: "All he saw with me was my past, while he told you about your future."

Hong Kong

The temples of Angkor Wat tell an ancient story.

When Mrs. Roosevelt was in Bangkok attending a meeting of
the World Federation of United Nations Associations, she was
invited by the Thai government to fly to Angkor Wat, the capital
of the ancient Khmer kingdom in nearby Cambodia. It was
then the monsoon season and the short excursion was seldom
free of rain, but this did not detract from Mrs. Roosevelt's
pleasure at seeing the famous jungle-bound city. We explored
richly ornamented palaces and temples, and studied serenely
sculptured religious figures. Mrs. Roosevelt was overwhelmed
by the scale of the city. It once encompassed six hundred temples, many of them now gripped by tree roots.

Cambodia

Bali's islanders captivate Mrs. Roosevelt.

Renowned for the beauty and serenity of its people, Bali did not disappoint Mrs. Roosevelt. She felt the entire island population was like a monastery's, every act of daily life influenced by religion. A fisherman brought his catch to a temple priest for a blessing. A stonecutter, repairing a road, started his day by building a little temple near his work and praying—and he ended his day's work with prayer.

Bali

In the communities we visited, villagers lived by rigid social customs, each person seeming to draw strength—and repose—from being part of the close-knit unit. At Ubud, Mrs. Roosevelt learned about traditional village ways from Prince Tjokorde Agung Sukawati, at left, who owns there an enclave of guest houses for travelers. Ubud is also noted for its skilled artists, none more supremely talented than dancers, like the lovely pair above, whose art is a looking-glass reflection of contemporary Balinese life.

Bali

In Belgium for a conference, Mrs. Roosevelt has a chance to explore some international showcases.

It was World's Fair time in Brussels when Mrs. Roosevelt visited the Belgian capital to participate in a conference of the World Federation of the United Nations Associations. At left, she visits the enormous Russian Pavilion dominated by a towering statue of Lenin. Above, at one of the World's Fair restaurants, she entertains the head of the Soviet delegation to W.F.U.N.A., who is sitting on her right with an interpreter beside her. Beyond the interpreter is Mrs. Roosevelt's secretary, Maureen Corr. Across the table from Mrs. Roosevelt is Harry Belafonte, whose concert at the U.S. Pavilion she had attended the night before.

Belgium

Soviet dancers offer an entertaining evening.

During her stay in Brussels, Mrs. Roosevelt was especially delighted to see a program of the Soviet Union's extraordinary Moiseyev dancers. Backstage after the performance she met and offered a toast to Mr. Igor Moiseyev (standing beside her) and his talented troupe.

Belgium

Mrs. Roosevelt takes time for some Belgian sight-seeing.

While in Brussels for meetings, Mrs. Roosevelt also went on excursions to cities beyond the capital. Here, in a Ghent museum, with her grandson, John, and my wife Edna, she studies some distinguished Flemish art. She particularly enjoyed this visit as my wife, who is an art authority, provided a knowledgeable commentary on the paintings.

Belgium

Next page: A Berlin synagogue finds an ally.

During a visit to West Berlin, Mrs. Roosevelt was so impressed by this ruined synagogue, an important landmark for German Jews that was destroyed by Nazis in 1938, she wrote about it in her column, "My Day." The resulting international publicity encouraged municipal authorities to begin an extensive program of restoration.

Berlin

Friends enjoy vacation time in Switzerland.

On a Swiss holiday, Mrs. Roosevelt enthusiastically indulges in some Swiss fun: a long sleigh ride on a clear winter morning. With Maureen Corr and my wife, we rode high up in the mountains above St. Moritz to have a leisurely lunch at a popular skiers' restaurant.

Switzerland

Mrs. Roosevelt and her secretary, Maureen Corr, stand by the Moskva River before the landmark symbol of the Soviet Union, the fancifully turreted and towered Kremlin.

On two trips to the Soviet Union, Mrs. Roosevelt covered thousands of miles and added hundreds of pieces to her travel jigsaw puzzle. She knew that traveling in a totalitarian country required careful planning to avoid being led only to official showplaces. She submitted requests to see as much as possible—in the capital, in Leningrad and other cities, even in a distant Soviet republic. Along with seeing some historic places, we studied two fields in depth—medical services and education—which brought considerable understanding of the overall scheme of Soviet endeavors.

U.S.S.R.

Soviet hospitality on both trips was prodigious. Almost by accident Mrs. Roosevelt learned that for each of her visits the furniture in her hotel suite in Moscow had been especially transported a thousand miles from Yalta: it was the same furniture her husband had used a dozen years earlier at the famous World War II Yalta Conference.

Next page: Mrs. Roosevelt lines up at Lenin's tomb.

For Soviets, the primary national shrine is Lenin's Mausoleum in the Kremlin's Red Square, and miles of people wait daily for the opportunity to see it. Mrs. Roosevelt insisted on taking her place in the line instead of being escorted directly to the tomb as our Intourist guide proposed.

U.S.S.R.

Above, Mrs. Roosevelt listens to a guide describing Lenin's apartment. At right, she chats with her interpreter, Anna Lavrova, before entering the Kremlin's Armory.

Among the grand palaces, domed cathedrals, and stately buildings encompassed within the walled Kremlin is the Armory, with its fabulous collection of imperial jewels, richly fashioned weapons, and other royal treasures. But no place in the Kremlin

U.S.S.R.

impressed Mrs. Roosevelt more than Lenin's small, plainly fur-
nished apartment. It is preserved exactly as Lenin knew it, to
the calendar on his desk which is open to the last day he sat
there. The arrangement of his conference table is still copied
in offices of present-day Soviet ministers and directors. Even
more striking, though, was our realization that whatever we
saw of Soviet life as we traveled through the U.S.S.R. had
emanated from this modest little study.

U.S.S.R.

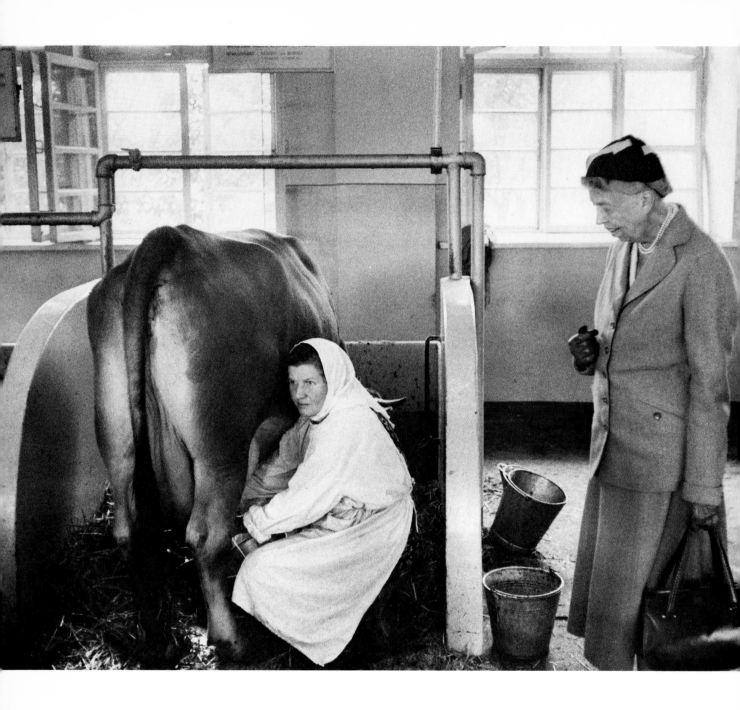

Mrs. Roosevelt inspects an agricultural showcase.

At a Moscow exhibition, farm produce from all over the Soviet Union was as meticulously displayed as the still life of apples, above. The peasant woman and her cow, at left, were brought to the capital because the cow had produced a record quantity of milk for one year. Because she had bred the cow, it was said that the woman was made a member of the Supreme Soviet, nominally the country's highest lawmaking body.

U.S.S.R.

Mrs. Roosevelt and Maureen Corr watch chess buffs.

Chess playing is a favorite pastime for Russians, and even some children of seven or eight are enviably expert. Here, contestants in the chess pavilion at Moscow's Gorki Park are typically absorbed in game strategy.

U.S.S.R.

With her interpreter, Anna Lavrova, standing beside her, Mrs. Roosevelt travels by subway.

Proud of their Moscow subway system, Russians show it enthusiastically to all foreigners. Mrs. Roosevelt was glad to take a ride and observe closely everyday Muscovites.

U.S.S.R.

A subway station becomes a sight-seeing marvel.

Like every other tourist who has seen Moscow's subway stations, Mrs. Roosevelt was amazed by their rich decor. With their vaulted ceilings, graceful arcades, lavish chandeliers, and bronze statues, the platforms are overwhelmingly grand.

U.S.S.R.

In Moscow, Mrs. Roosevelt meets the Deputy Minister of Health, above, on her right. On the roof of the University of Moscow, at right, she stands with the Director, who is the man beside her.

Pursuing her interests in medical services and education, Mrs. Roosevelt has detailed discussions with officials in these fields. These talks customarily take place around conference tables, like the one above, which are generously laden with cookies, candies, soft drinks, and fruit.

U.S.S.R.

Above, Mrs. Roosevelt walks with the staff of a Moscow psychiatric hospital. At right, she watches doctors at work in a Leningrad pediatric hospital.

While studying medical services, Mrs. Roosevelt learned that most Soviet doctors are women, as is evident in the pictures here. Full professors and heads of scientific institutions, however, usually are men. The professor to the right of Mrs. Roosevelt in the baby hospital is a notable exception.

U.S.S.R.

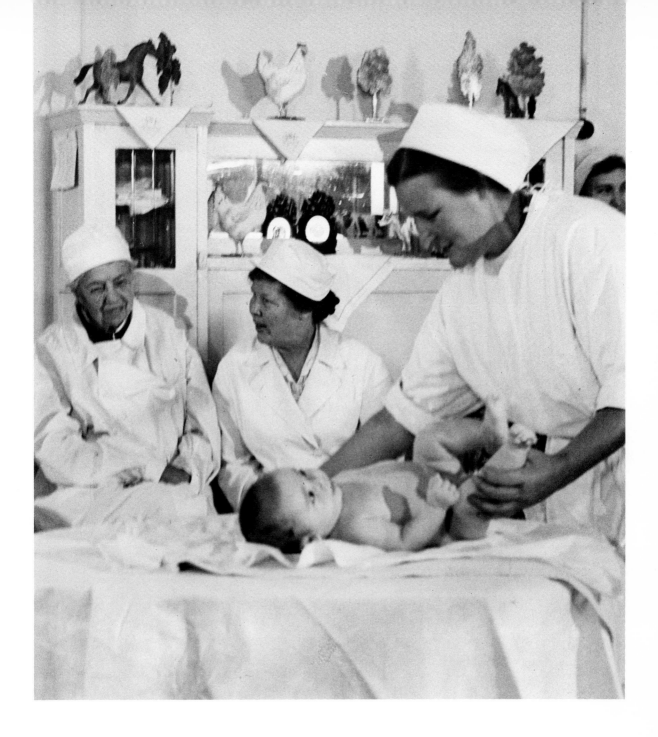

On one occasion we were in a hospital operating room where eight or nine operations were being performed simultaneously. All of us in surgical dress, we moved from table to table and were told about the operations being performed. At the last table a young woman, under local anesthesia, was undergoing abdominal surgery. A nurse whispered to her that the tall lady watching the procedure was Mrs. Franklin Delano Roosevelt. With her abdomen wide open, the woman nearly fell off the table in her eagerness to shake Mrs. Roosevelt's hand.

U.S.S.R.

Mrs. Roosevelt arrives at Moscow's Indian Embassy.

This occasion was preceded by a series of events that put me in the center of a diplomatic incident. We had just arrived in Moscow from a strenuous journey to one of the Soviet republics where, the night before, Mrs. Roosevelt had taken ill. I reproached myself for not delaying the trip, and when we arrived at the hotel suite Mrs. Roosevelt called off a government reception in her honor and went straight to bed.

While she was asleep, the telephone rang in the living room and I answered it. Someone wanted to speak to Mrs. Roosevelt. I said that she was not well and was sleeping. I was then told that it was Chairman Khrushchev's office. I said I was very

sorry but Mrs. Roosevelt could not be disturbed. After a pause, another voice on the phone said, "Mr. Gurewitsch, you are speaking to the Chairman, and I would like to speak to Mrs. Roosevelt." My answer was, "Sir, you are speaking to Mrs. Roosevelt's physician, and I am answering that Mrs. Roosevelt is not able to come to the telephone." His call concerned his reception that afternoon. Still reproaching myself for not postponing the arduous flight, I was firm that Mrs. Roosevelt could not be disturbed.

To make diplomatic matters even worse, when Mrs. Roosevelt awoke from her uninterrupted sleep, she felt much refreshed and ready to continue whatever was scheduled next. It was the dinner at the Indian Embassy.

Leningraders warmly receive Mrs. Roosevelt.

At left, Mrs. Roosevelt arrives in Leningrad as a member of the delegation of the American Association for the United Nations to attend a meeting with its Soviet counterpart; she is cordially welcomed at the railroad station. Above, flanked by Soviet and American delegates, she addresses the joint meeting of the two organizations.

U.S.S.R.

Leningrad's river panorama draws an appreciative audience.

Like Moscow, Leningrad straddles a spectacularly sweeping waterway. Here Mrs. Roosevelt, with Soviet sightseers curiously watching her, admired Leningrad vistas from the banks of the Neva River. She was impressed that there were few signs of the terrible nine-hundred-day bombardment that the city endured during World War II.

U.S.S.R.

Above, Mrs. Roosevelt stands before Leningrad's Winter Palace. Right, with my wife Edna, she leaves the Peter and Paul prison museum where the seated woman has just asked incredulously, "Is this Mrs. Roosevelt?"

With her great regard for history and the lessons it teaches, Mrs. Roosevelt was deeply impressed at being in the enormous square in front of the Winter Palace where the 1917 Soviet revolution began. History was also recorded at the Peter and Paul museum. Originally built as a fortress to protect Leningrad from seaward invasion, it later became a grim czarist stronghold for political prisoners that included the celebrated writers Feodor Dostoyevsky and Maxim Gorki.

U.S.S.R.

146

Lenin's tank invites careful study.

Mrs. Roosevelt was especially fascinated with this monumental relic at the Winter Palace. Lenin rode in the tank as leader of the revolutionary crowd that assaulted the czarist residence and changed the course of history.

U.S.S.R.

Another Roosevelt Yalta Conference.

At Yalta, we were driven to the Khrushchev villa. There were several security checks along the way, and at one point, we stopped in a wooded area for no apparent reason. We just sat there, making the punctual Mrs. Roosevelt nervous. But this turned out to be a necessary delay so we would arrive at the villa exactly on time. The moment we drove up, the Khrushchev family—the Chairman and his wife, their daughter, and son-in-law—was standing in front of the house ready to welcome Mrs. Roosevelt. After warm greetings, Mr. Khrushchev showed us his flower gardens and the lovely view of Yalta. Then he sat down with Mrs. Roosevelt and her interpreter, Anna Lavrova, above, for a long conversation.

U.S.S.R.

A step toward Soviet-American understanding.

Mrs. Roosevelt's discussion with Mr. Khrushchev lasted over three hours and covered many topics. Mr. Khrushchev was always pleasant, but he would not budge on any ideological point. When I took the picture above, he was saying, "As certain as it takes nine months to make a baby, as certainly communism will rule the world."

We enjoyed a relaxed family meal and later, when we were about to leave, Mr. Khrushchev asked Mrs. Roosevelt whether he could tell the newspapers that they had had a friendly conversation. Her answer was: "We had a friendly conversation but we differed." Mr. Khrushchev smiled and said, "At least we didn't shoot at each other."

After the interview, Mrs. Roosevelt told me how impressed she was by Mr. Khrushchev's powerful personality. She said that throughout their conversation she had tried to think who in the Western world could match him. As a listener to their talks, I felt she herself had been an admirable match.

U.S.S.R.

152

Above, the Mufti of Samarkand welcomes Mrs. Roosevelt with presents. Right, she visits the ruins of a splendidly tiled mosque built by Tamerlane.

All her life Mrs. Roosevelt had wanted to see Samarkand, the legendary Central Asian city sacked by Genghis Khan and rebuilt by Tamerlane. As the capital of Tamerlane's far-flung empire, Samarkand was once a rich center of art and learning, with lavishly ornamented buildings. For Mrs. Roosevelt, the city's reminders of its ancient past had an incomparable romantic aura. Along with the Taj Mahal and the Khyber Pass, it was the third place that years ago her father had written her that she should one day visit.

U.S.S.R.

Mrs. Roosevelt died on November 7, 1962,
several months after the picture on the left was taken.

She was mourned around the world—by those
who knew her and by those who only knew of her.

She has become a legend of a true spirit of humanity,
of selflessness, of the high standards of behavior that
are attainable by everyone.

She is still the First Lady of the World.

Universal Declaration of Human Rights

Preamble

Whereas recognition of the inherent dignity and of the equal and inalienable rights of all members of the human family is the foundation of freedom, justice and peace in the world,

Whereas disregard and contempt for human rights have resulted in barbarous acts which have outraged the conscience of mankind, and the advent of a world in which human beings shall enjoy freedom of speech and belief and freedom from fear and want has been proclaimed as the highest aspiration of the common people,

Whereas it is essential, if man is not to be compelled to have recourse, as a last resort, to rebellion against tyranny and oppression, that human rights should be protected by the rule of law,

Whereas it is essential to promote the development of friendly relations between nations,

Whereas the peoples of the United Nations have in the Charter reaffirmed their faith in fundamental human rights, in the dignity and worth of the human person and in the equal rights of men and women and have determined to promote social progress and better standards of life in larger freedom,

Whereas Member States have pledged themselves to achieve, in co-operation with the United Nations, the promotion of universal respect for and observance of human rights and fundamental freedoms,

Whereas a common understanding of these rights and freedoms is of the greatest importance for the full realization of this pledge,

Now, Therefore,

The General Assembly

proclaims

The Universal Declaration of Human Rights as a common standard of achievement for all peoples and all nations, to the end that every individual and every organ of society, keeping this Declaration constantly in mind, shall strive by teaching and education to promote respect for these rights and freedoms and by progressive measures, national and international, to secure their universal and effective recognition and observance, both among the peoples of Member States themselves and among the peoples of territories under their jurisdiction.

Article 1. All human beings are born free and equal in dignity and rights. They are endowed with reason and conscience and should act towards one another in a spirit of brotherhood.

Article 2. Everyone is entitled to all the rights and freedoms set forth in this Declaration, without distinction of any kind, such as race, colour, sex, language, religion, political or other opinion, national or social origin, property, birth or other status.

Furthermore, no distinction shall be made on the basis of the political, jurisdictional or international status of the country or territory to which a person belongs, whether it be independent, trust, non-self-governing or under any other limitation of sovereignty.

Article 3. Everyone has the right to life, liberty and security of person.

Article 4. No one shall be held in slavery or servitude; slavery and the slave trade shall be prohibited in all their forms.

Article 5. No one shall be subjected to torture or to cruel, inhuman or degrading treatment or punishment.

Article 6. Everyone has the right to recognition everywhere as a person before the law.

Article 7. All are equal before the law and are entitled without any discrimination to equal protection of the law. All are entitled to equal protection against any discrimination in violation of this Declaration and against any incitement to such discrimination.

Article 8. Everyone has the right to an effective remedy by the competent national tribunals for acts violating the fundamental rights granted him by the constitution or by law.

Article 9. No one shall be subjected to arbitrary arrest, detention or exile.

Article 10. Everyone is entitled in full equality to a fair and public hearing by an independent and impartial tribunal, in the determination of his rights and obligations and of any criminal charge against him.

Article 11. (1) Everyone charged with a penal offence has the right to be presumed innocent until proved guilty according to law in a public trial at which he has had all the guarantees necessary for his defence.

(2) No one shall be held guilty of any penal offence on account of any act or omission which did not constitute a penal offence, under national or international law, at the time when it was committed. Nor shall a heavier penalty be imposed than the one that was applicable at the time the penal offence was committed.

Article 12. No one shall be subjected to arbitrary interference with his privacy, family, home or correspondence, nor to attacks upon his honour and reputation. Everyone has the right to the protection of the law against such interference or attacks.

Article 13. (1) Everyone has the right to freedom of movement and residence within the borders of each state.

(2) Everyone has the right to leave any country, including his own, and to return to his country.

Article 14. (1) Everyone has the right to seek and to enjoy in other countries asylum from persecution.

(2) This right may not be invoked in the case of prosecutions genuinely arising from non-political crimes or from acts contrary to the purposes and principles of the United Nations.

Article 15. (1) Everyone has the right to a nationality.

(2) No one shall be arbitrarily deprived of his nationality nor denied the right to change his nationality.

Article 16. (1) Men and women of full age, without any limitation due to race, nationality or religion, have the right to marry and to found a family. They are entitled to equal rights as to marriage, during marriage and at its dissolution.

(2) Marriage shall be entered into only with the free and full consent of the intending spouses.

(3) The family is the natural and fundamental group unit of society and is entitled to protection by society and the State.

Article 17. (1) Everyone has the right to own property alone as well as in association with others.

(2) No one shall be arbitrarily deprived of his property.

Article 18. Everyone has the right to freedom of thought, conscience and religion; this right includes freedom to change his religion or belief, and freedom, either alone or in community with others and in public or private, to manifest his religion or belief in teaching, practice, worship and observance.

Article 19. Everyone has the right to freedom of opinion and expression; this right includes freedom to hold opinions without interference and to seek, receive and impart information and ideas through any media and regardless of frontiers.

Article 20. (1) Everyone has the right to freedom of peaceful assembly and association.

(2) No one may be compelled to belong to an association.

Article 21. (1) Everyone has the right to take part in the government of his country, directly or through freely chosen representatives.

(2) Everyone has the right of equal access to public service in his country.

(3) The will of the people shall be the basis of the authority of government; this will shall be expressed in periodic and genuine elections which shall be by universal and equal suffrage and shall be held by secret vote or by equivalent free voting procedures.

Article 22. Everyone, as a member of society, has the right to social security and is entitled to realization, through national effort and international co-operation and in accordance with the organization and resources of each State, of the economic, social and cultural rights indispensable for his dignity and the free development of his personality.

Article 23. (1) Everyone has the right to work, to free choice of employment, to just and favourable conditions of work and to protection against unemployment.

(2) Everyone, without any discrimination, has the right to equal pay for equal work.

(3) Everyone who works has the right to just and favourable remuneration ensuring for himself and his family an existence worthy of human dignity, and supplemented, if necessary, by other means of social protection.

(4) Everyone has the right to form and to join trade unions for the protection of his interests.

Article 24. Everyone has the right to rest and leisure, including reasonable limitation of working hours and periodic holidays with pay.

Article 25. (1) Everyone has the right to a standard of living adequate for the health and well-being of himself and of his family, including food, clothing, housing and medical care and necessary social services, and the right to security in the event of unemployment, sickness, disability, widowhood, old age or other lack of livelihood in circumstances beyond his control.

(2) Motherhood and childhood are entitled to special care and assistance. All children, whether born in or out of wedlock, shall enjoy the same social protection.

Article 26. (1) Everyone has the right to education. Education shall be free, at least in the elementary and fundamental stages. Elementary education shall be compulsory. Technical and professional education shall be made generally available and higher education shall be equally accessible to all on the basis of merit.

(2) Education shall be directed to the full development of the human personality and to the strengthening of respect for human rights and fundamental freedoms. It shall promote understanding, tolerance and friendship among all nations, racial or religious groups, and shall further the activities of the United Nations for the maintenance of peace.

(3) Parents have a prior right to choose the kind of education that shall be given to their children.

Article 27. (1) Everyone has the right freely to participate in the cultural life of the community, to enjoy the arts and to share in scientific advancement and its benefits.

(2) Everyone has the right to the protection of the moral and material interests resulting from any scientific, literary or artistic production of which he is the author.

Article 28. Everyone is entitled to a social and international order in which the rights and freedoms set forth in this Declaration can be fully realized.

Article 29. (1) Everyone has duties to the community in which alone the free and full development of his personality is possible.

(2) In the exercise of his rights and freedoms, everyone shall be subject only to such limitations as are determined by law solely for the purpose of securing due recognition and respect for the rights and freedoms of others and of meeting the just requirements of morality, public order and the general welfare in a democratic society.

(3) These rights and freedoms may in no case be exercised contrary to the purposes and principles of the United Nations.

Article 30. Nothing in this Declaration may be interpreted as implying for any State, group or person any right to engage in any activity or to perform any act aimed at the destruction of any of the rights and freedoms set forth herein.

*This token of my love and admiration
for Mrs. Roosevelt is shared by my wife Edna,
who joined me in countless hours of recollecting
our experiences with Mrs. Roosevelt.*

Notes about the Author

A. David Gurewitsch, New York physician and specialist in rehabilitation medicine, has been a teacher at Columbia Presbyterian Medical Center for thirty-four years, rising to the position of clinical professor, attending physician and consultant. Since 1952 he has been medical director (presently medical director emeritus) at Blythedale Children's Hospital in Valhalla, New York. Dr. Gurewitsch was first medical officer of the United Nations for several years and has served on a panel of advisors to the Secretary of Health, Education and Welfare in Washington. He has published in scientific journals. Among his many other activities, Dr. Gurewitsch has served on the hospital ship, *Hope,* and has been a United States delegate to the World Federation of United Nations Associations meetings in Bangkok, Geneva, Brussels, Warsaw and New Delhi. Dr. Gurewitsch was Mrs. Roosevelt's personal physician for sixteen years—from the time she left the White House.

Born in Zurich, Switzerland, of Russian parents, Dr. Gurewitsch has made his home in New York with his wife and two daughters.

Picture credits: Leo Rosenthal, pages 10–29/Maureen Corr, pages 31 and 88/Government of India, pages 93 and 95/Robert Mühlstock, page 98/Henry Grossman, page 100/Government of U.S.S.R., page 128.

**All other photographs were taken by, and are the property of,
A. David Gurewitsch, M.D.**